Pre-K

Hooked on Phonics®

Letter Sounds

Designed and illustrated by

Big Yellow Taxi, Inc.

Letter Sounds

Say the name of each thing out loud.
Listen for the sound of the letter in the word.

m	t
n	u
o	v
p	w
q	x
r	y
s	z

m

Look at the pictures. Point to the letter "m."
Listen for the m sound as you say each word out loud.

moon

monkey

mushroom

Merry m

I did it!

Say the name of each thing out loud.
Circle the things that begin with the m sound.

n

Look at the pictures. Point to the letter "n."
Listen for the **n** sound as you say each word out loud.

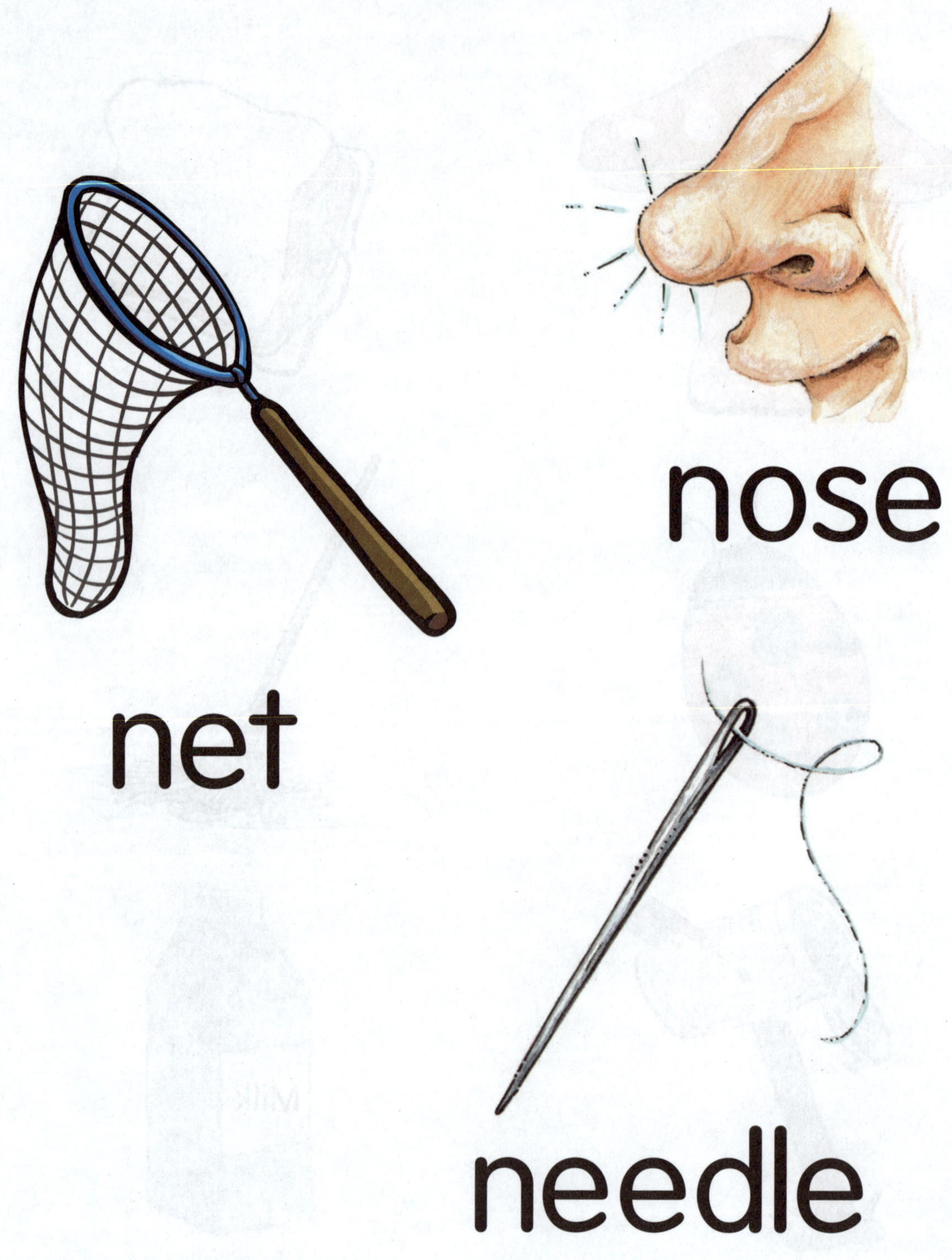

Nifty n

Say the name of each thing out loud.
Color the things that begin with the **n** sound.

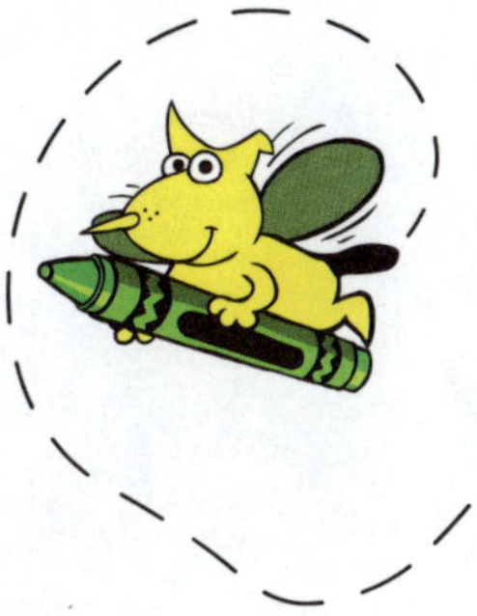

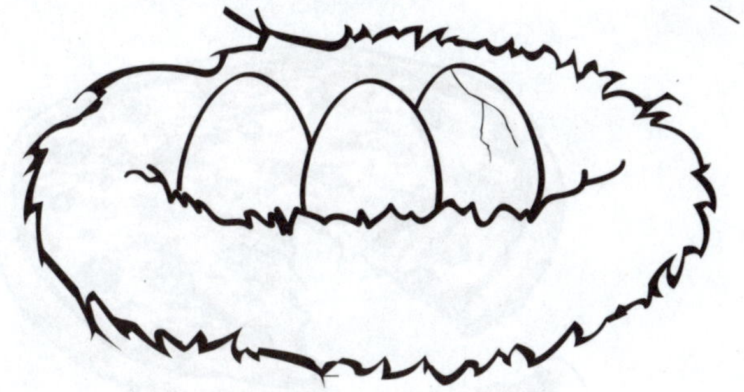

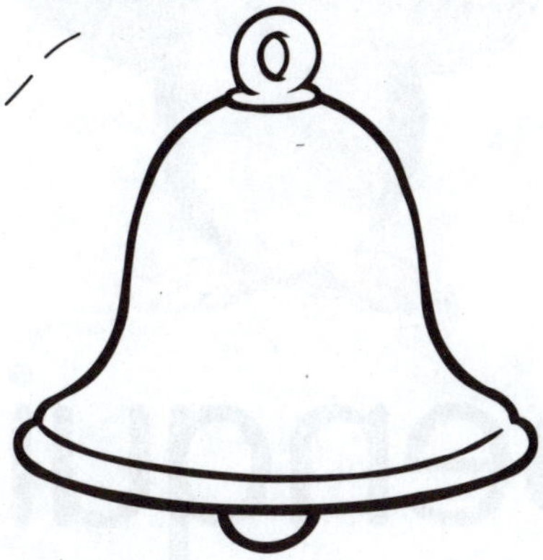

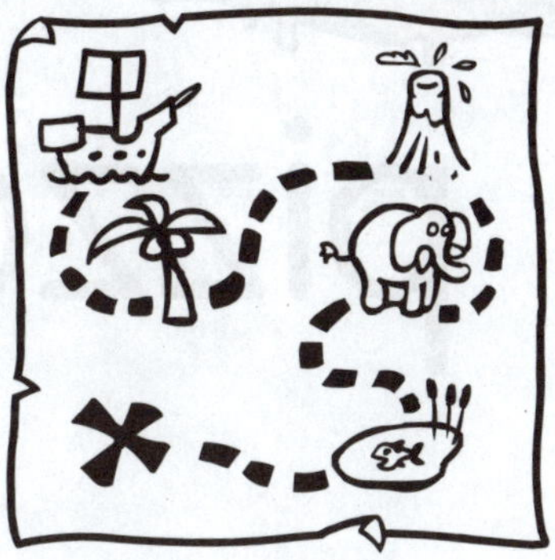

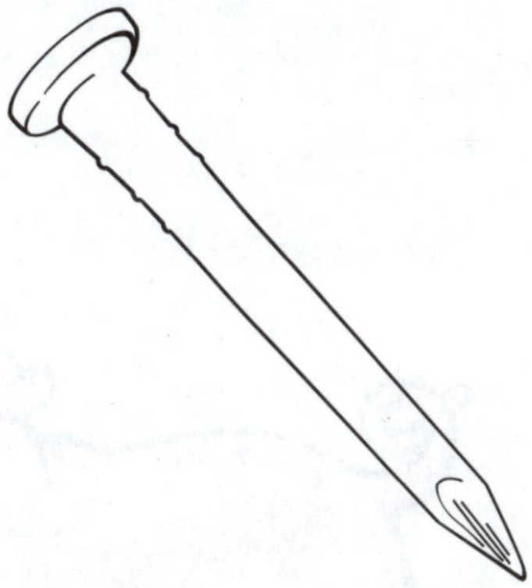

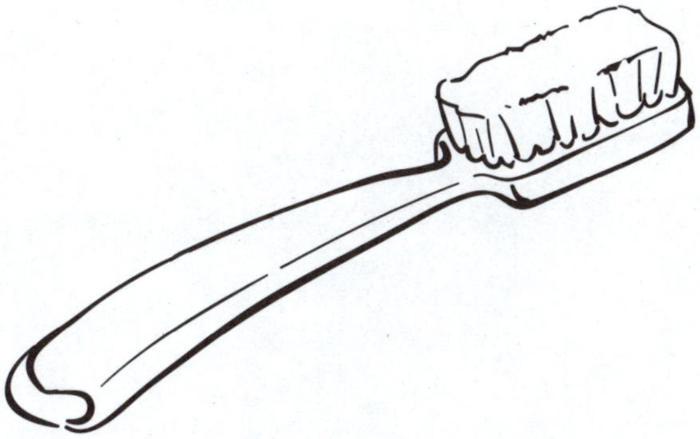

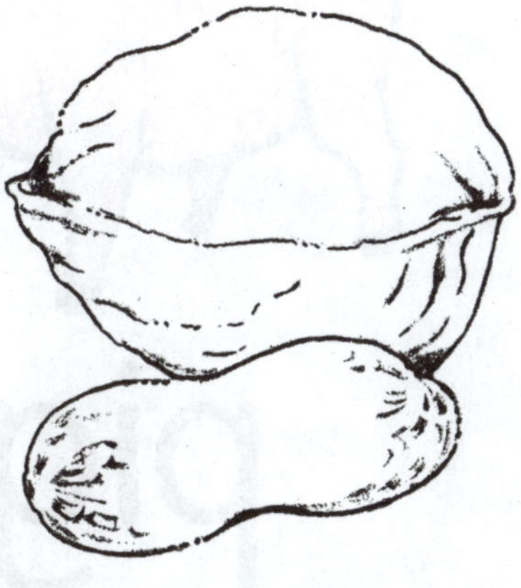

p

Look at the pictures. Point to the letter "p."
Listen for the **p** sound as you say each word out loud.

penguin

pizza

pig

Perfect p

Help Pop Fox get the pig to its pen.
Draw a path through the things that begin with the **p** sound.

START

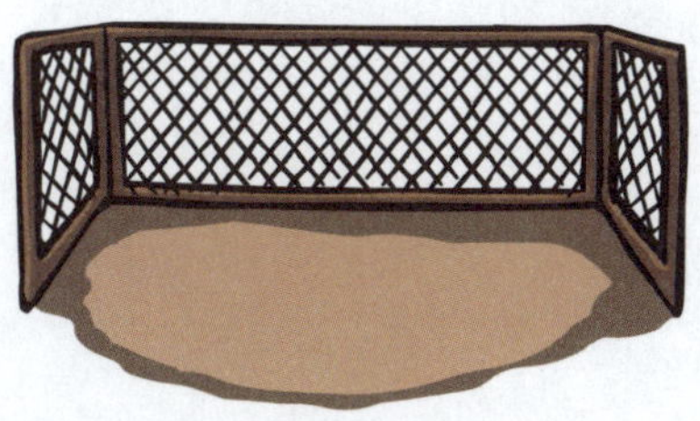

b

Look at the pictures. Point to the letter "b."
Listen for the b sound as you say each word out loud.

ball

bird

butterfly

Buzzing b

Say the name of the things in each row out loud.
Circle the two things that begin with the **b** sound.

h

Look at the pictures. Point to the letter "h."
Listen for the h sound as you say each word out loud.

horse

hat

helicopter

Happy h

I did it!

Say the name of each thing out loud.
Color the things that begin with the **h** sound.

Look at the pictures. Point to the letter "w."
Listen for the **w** sound as you say each word out loud.

wagon

watch

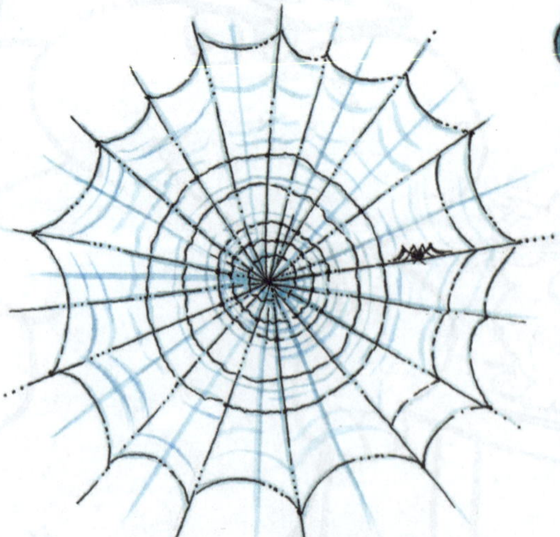

web

Wiggly w

Say the name of each thing out loud.
Color the things that begin with the w sound.

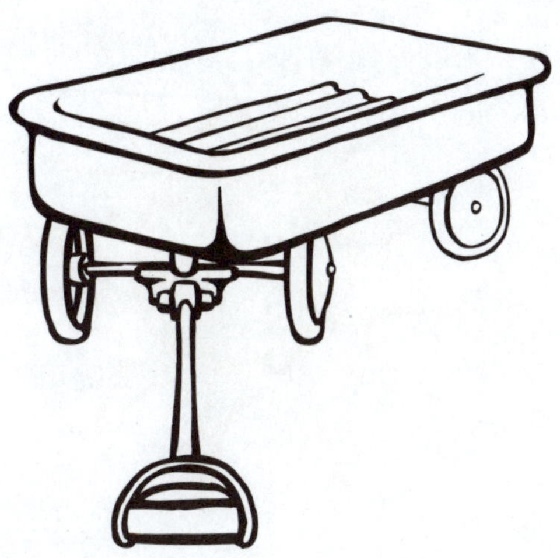

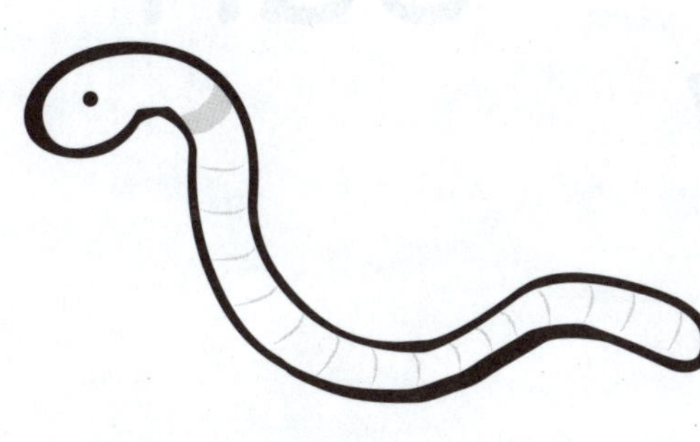

Look at the pictures. Point to the letter "s."
Listen for the s sound as you say each word out loud.

sun

seal

sandal

Silly s

Say the name of each thing out loud.
Circle the things that begin with the s sound.

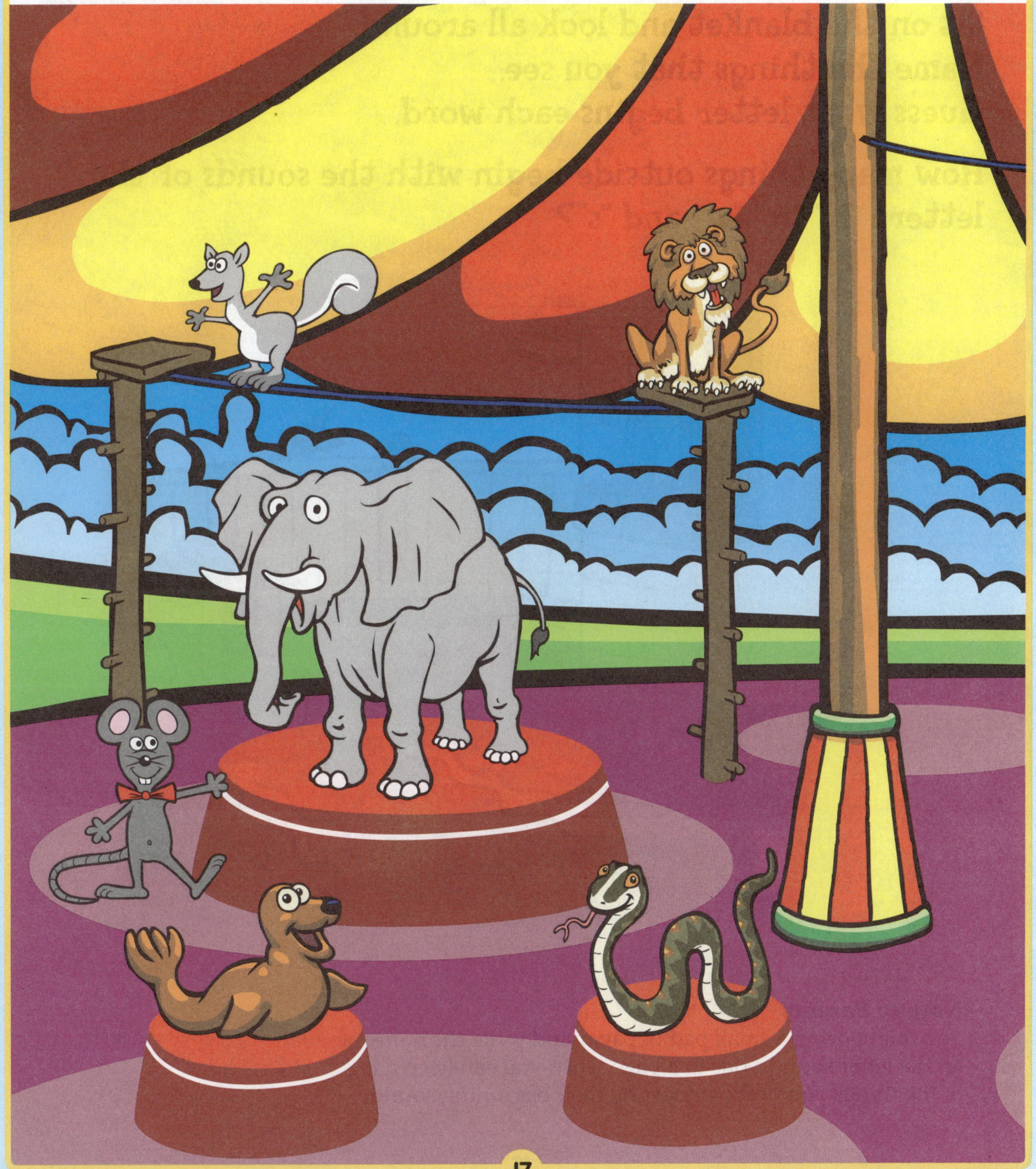

Searching for Sounds

Put a blanket on the ground outdoors.

Sit on the blanket and look all around.
Name the things that you see.
Guess what letter begins each word.

How many things outside begin with the sounds of the letters "b," "h," "w," and "s"?

Note to Parents
You might bring a small pad of paper and write the name of all the letter sounds, one to a page. Then you can keep a log of the things you find outdoors by their beginning sound.

When you're cleaning up, say the name of one of the toys.

Label some of the things in your room with the beginning sounds of their names, such as "b" for books and "t" for toy chest.

Note to Parents
Learning to listen for and separate the sounds in words is just as important as being able to recognize the letters on a page. You can help your child practice this skill by stretching out the sounds of words that you see around you, such as on store signs or packaging in your home.

Look at the pictures. Point to the letter "c."
Listen for the c sound as you say each word out loud.

cookie

cat

carrot

Clever c

Say the name of each thing out loud.
Color the things that begin with the c sound.

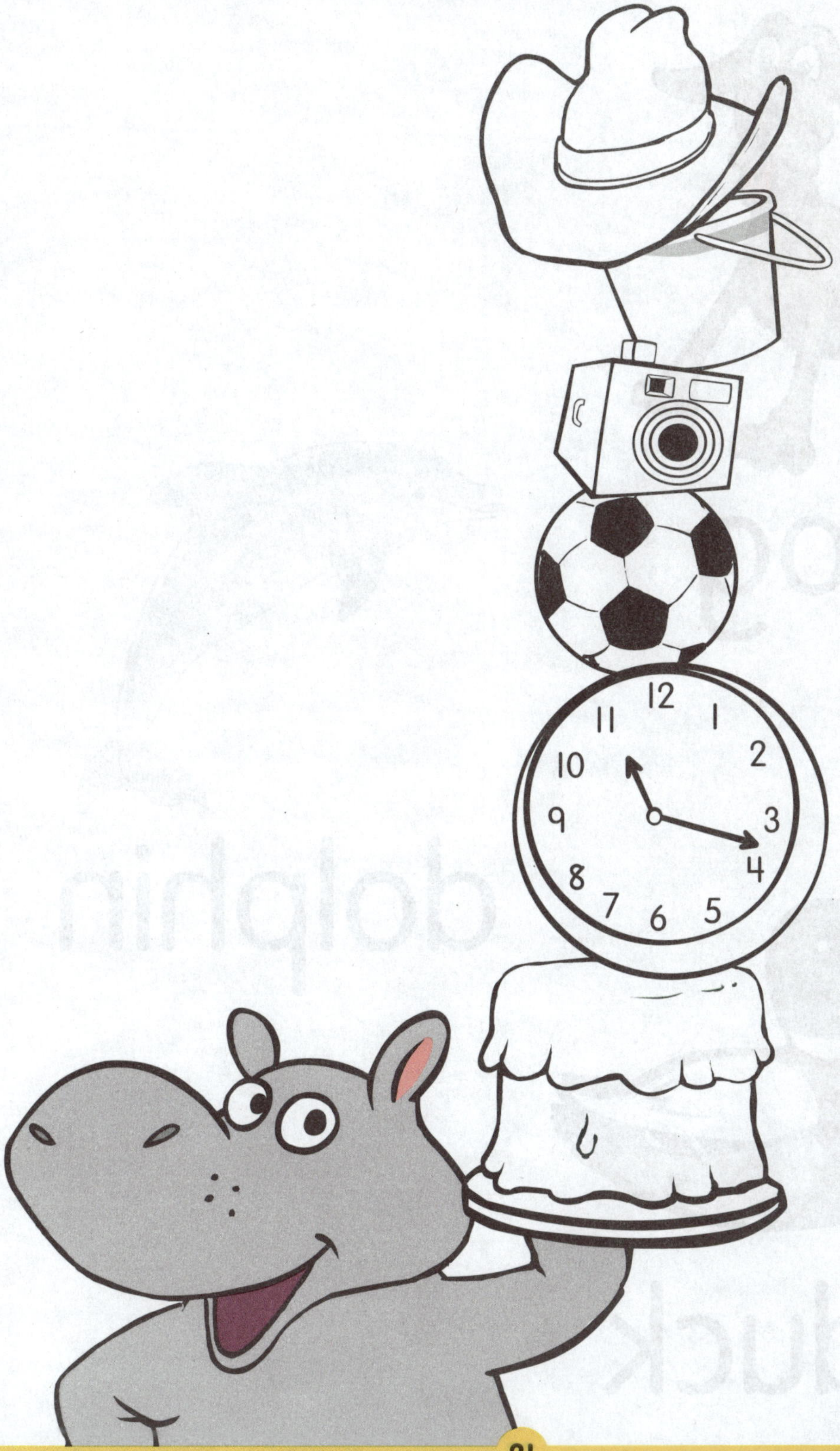

d

Look at the pictures. Point to the letter "d."
Listen for the d sound as you say each word out loud.

dog

dolphin

duck

Daffy d

I did it!

Say the name of each thing out loud.
Circle the things that begin with the **d** sound.

Look at the pictures. Point to the letter "f."
Listen for the f sound as you say each word out loud.

Friendly f

Help Pop Fox find his friend Hip-O.
Draw a path through the things that begin with the **f** sound.

g

Look at the pictures. Point to the letter "g."
Listen for the g sound as you say each word out loud.

guitar

goat

garbage

Giggly g

Say the name of each thing out loud.
Color the things that begin with the g sound.

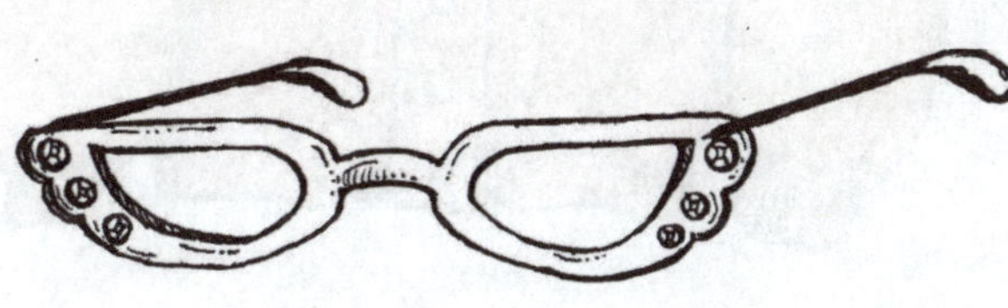

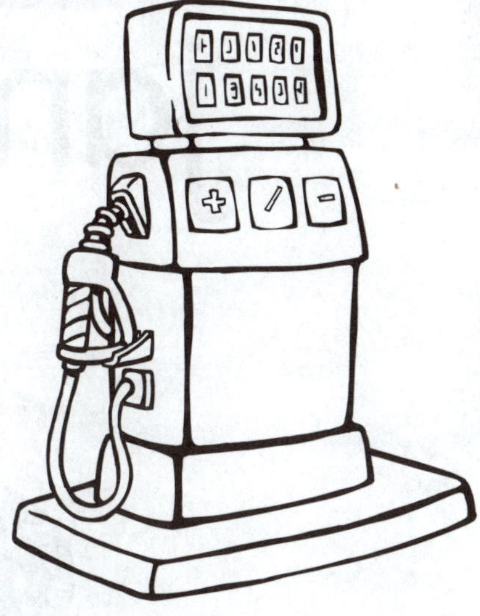

Look at the pictures. Point to the letter "j."
Listen for the j sound as you say each word out loud.

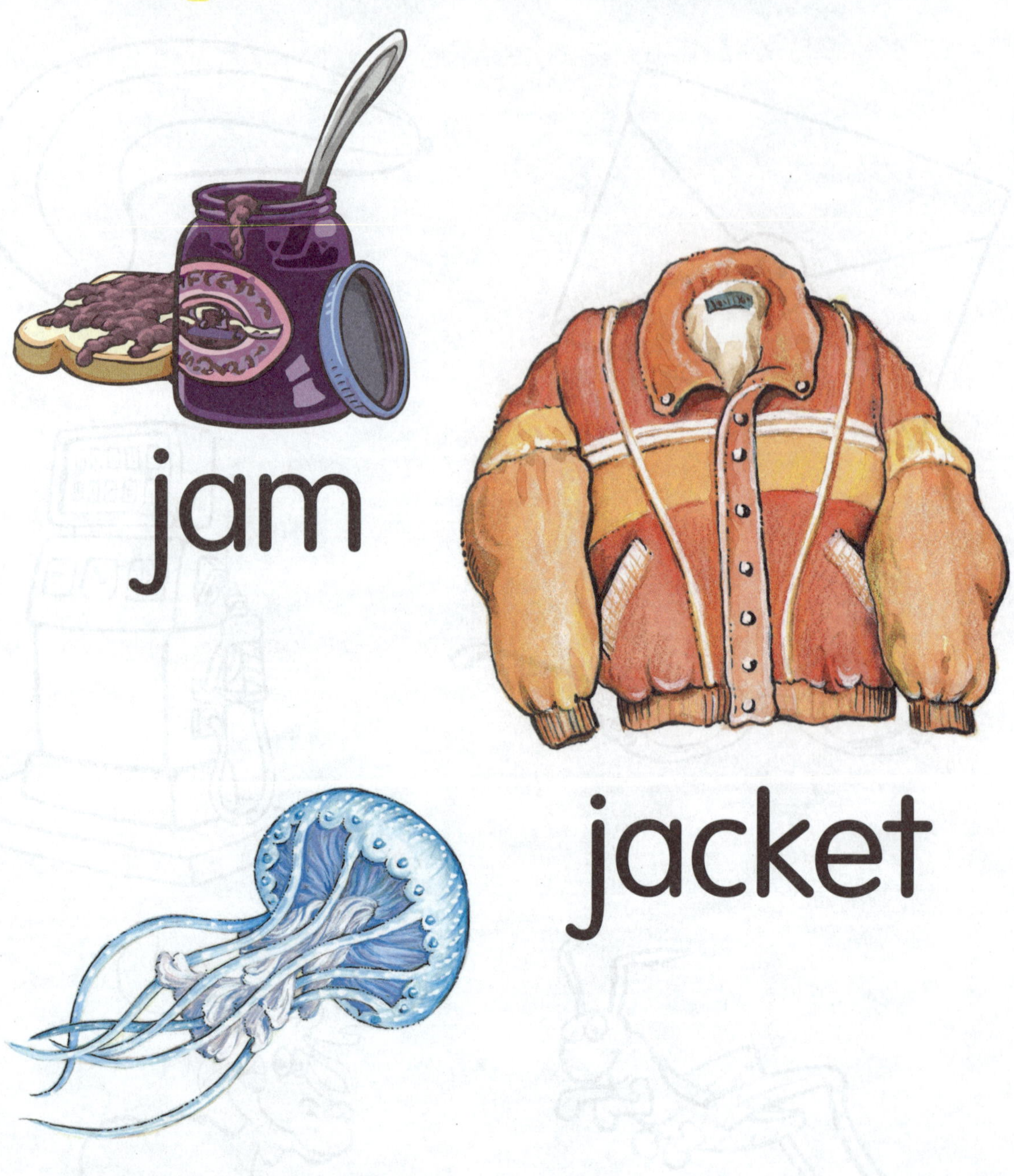

jam

jacket

jellyfish

Jiggly j

Say the name of each thing out loud.
Circle the things that begin with the j sound.

k

Look at the pictures. Point to the letter "K."
Listen for the k sound as you say each word out loud.

Kicky K

Where is Hip-O's Kite?
Draw a path through the things that begin with the k sound.

l

Look at the pictures. Point to the letter "l."
Listen for the l sound as you say each word out loud.

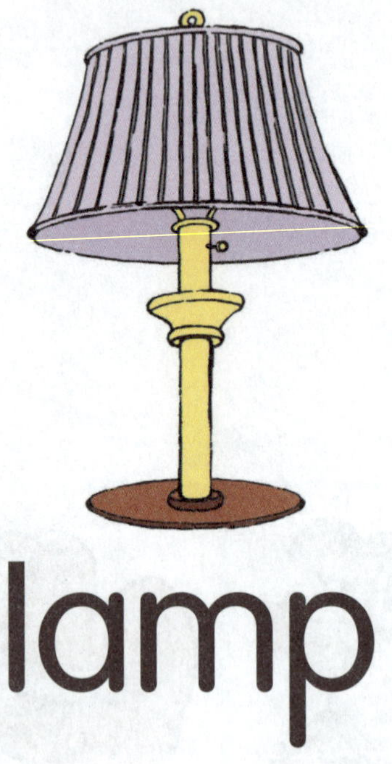

lamp

lion

lemon

Lucky l

Say the name of each thing out loud.
Circle the things that begin with the l sound.

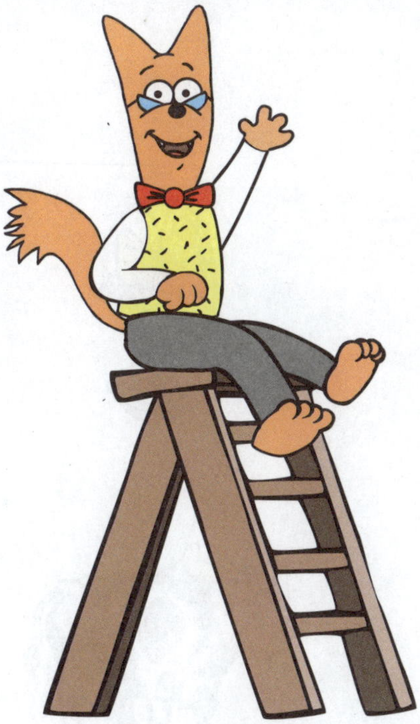

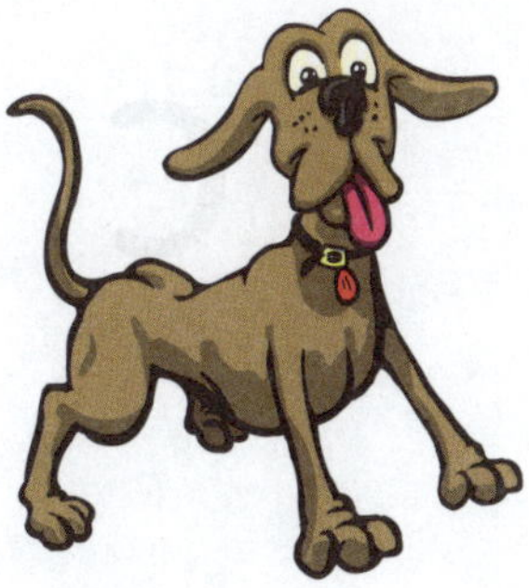

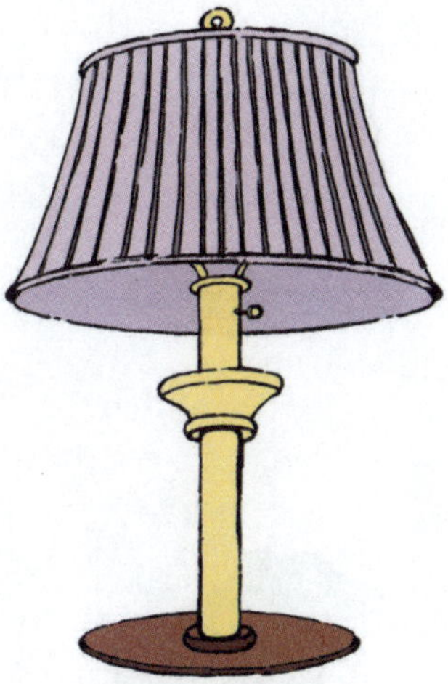

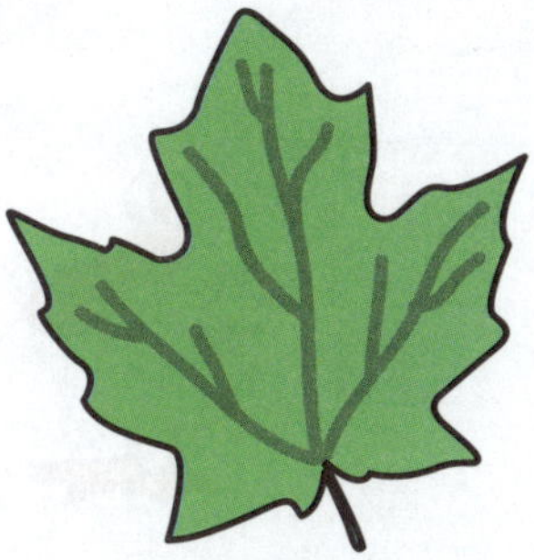

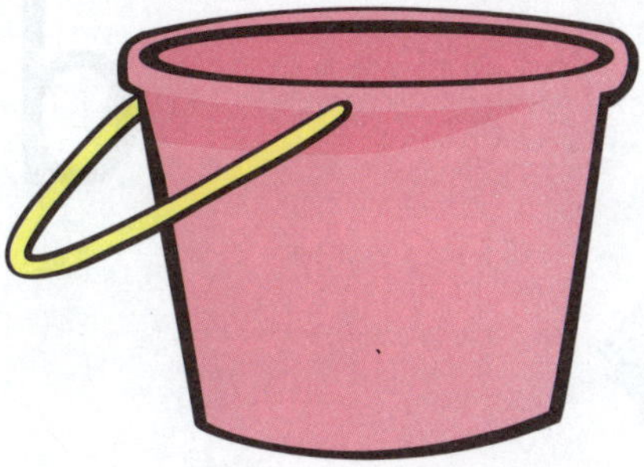

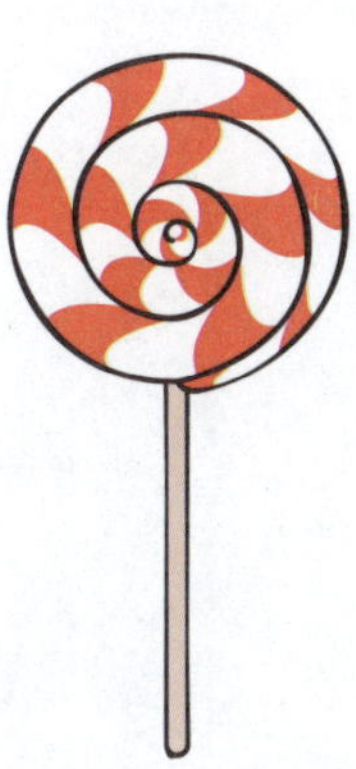

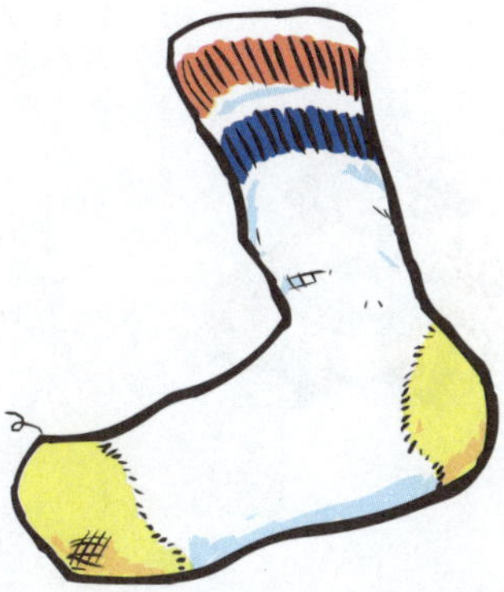

That's a Match

Say the name of each thing out loud.
Draw a line to match each thing to the letter that begins its name.

c

d

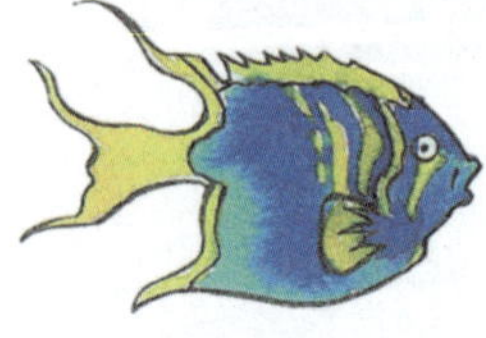

f

Match Maker

Say the name of each thing out loud.
Draw a line to match each thing to the letter that begins its name.

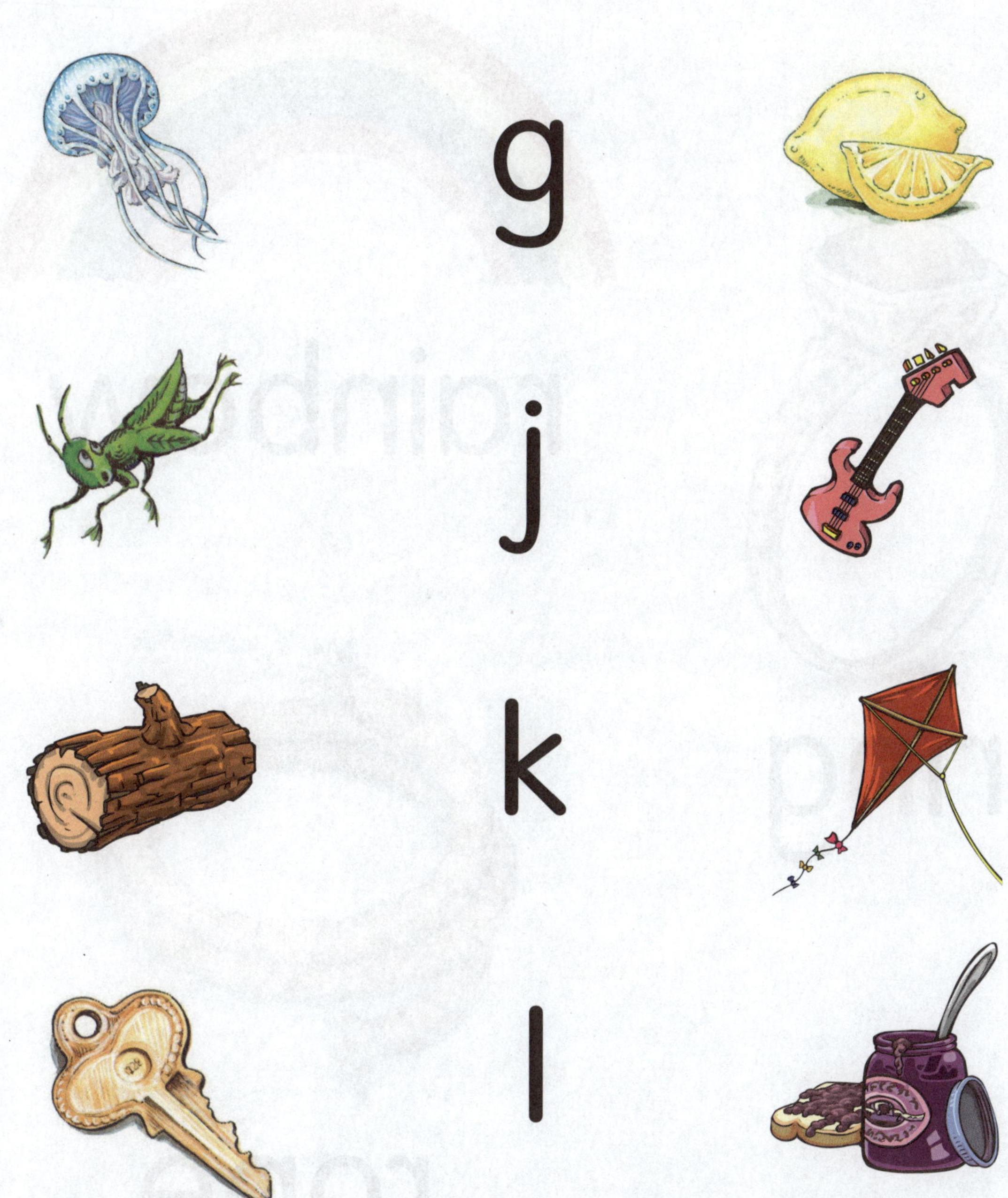

Look at the pictures. Point to the letter "r."
Listen for the r sound as you say each word out loud.

rainbow

ring

rope

Really r

Say the name of the things in each row out loud.
Circle the two things that begin with the r sound.

Look at the pictures. Point to the letter "t."
Listen for the t sound as you say each word out loud.

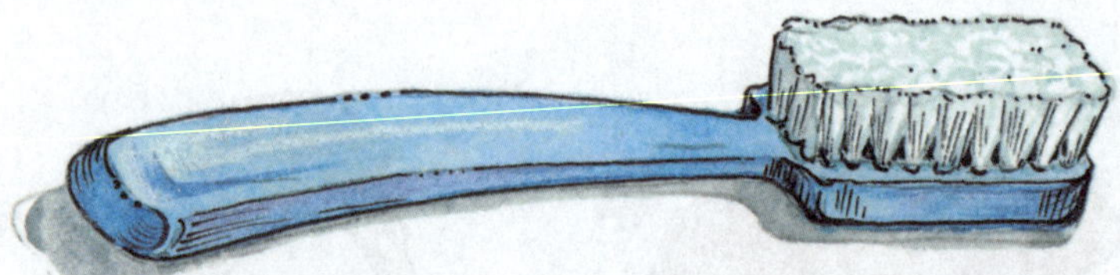

toothbrush

turtle

tiger

Terrific t

Say the name of each thing out loud.
Color the things that begin with the t sound.

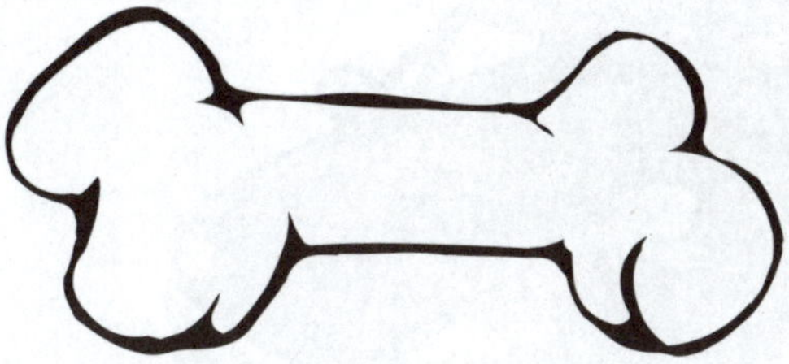

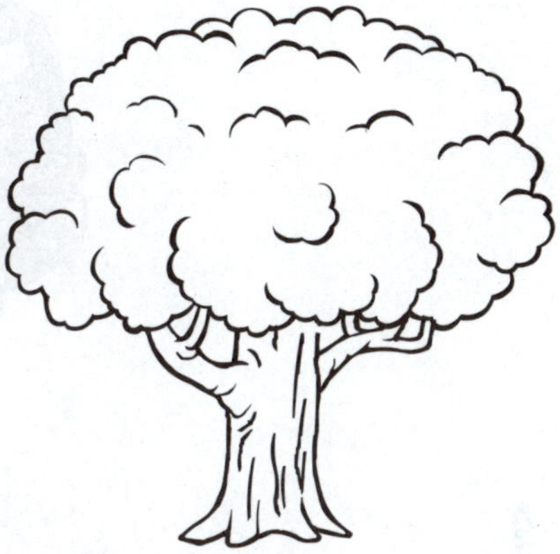

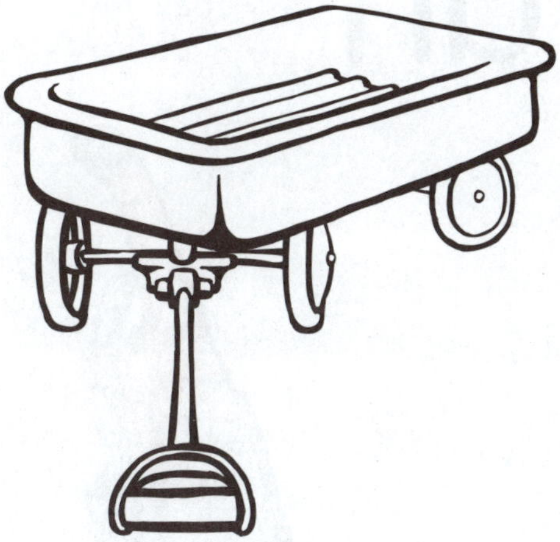

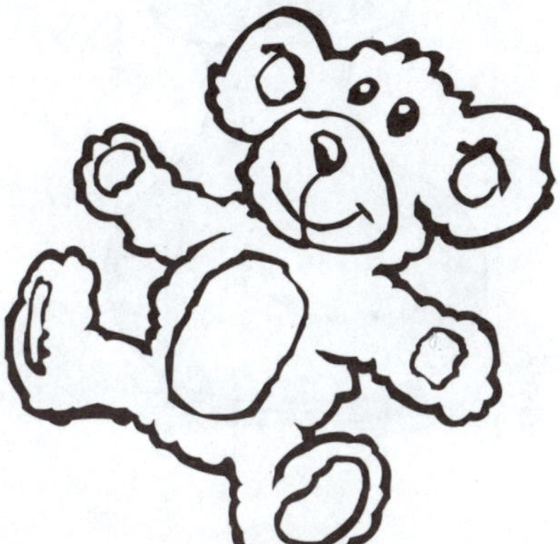

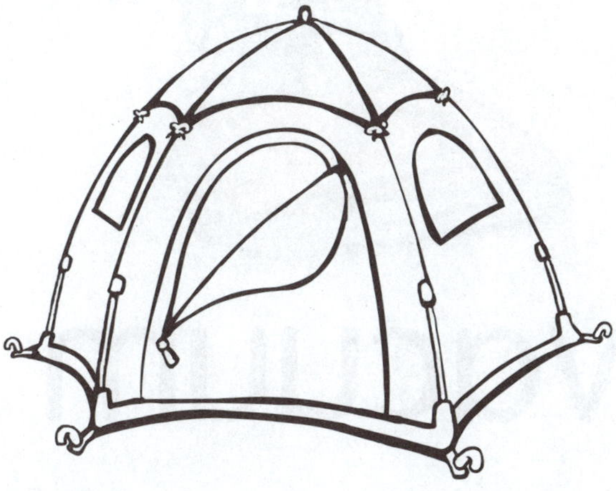

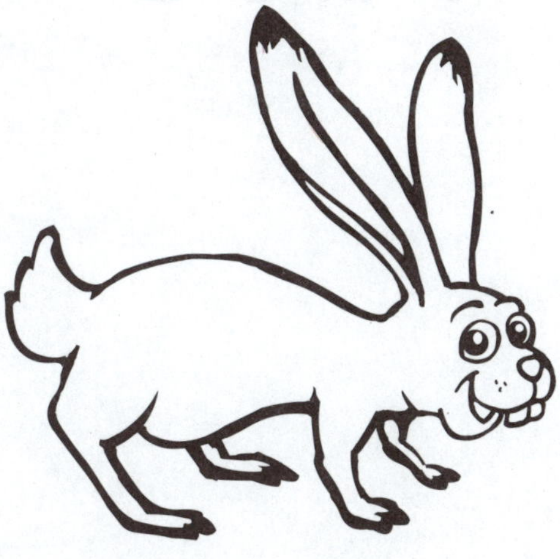

v

Look at the pictures. Point to the letter "v."
Listen for the **v** sound as you say each word out loud.

van

vase

vacuum

Very v

Help Hip-O get to the van.
Draw a path through the things that begin with the **v** sound.

q

Look at the pictures. Point to the letter "q."
Listen for the q sound as you say each word out loud.

queen

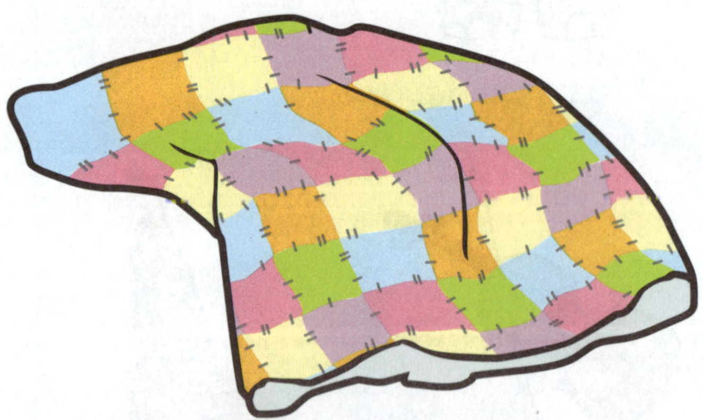

quilt

quarter

Quiet q

Say the name of each thing out loud.
Circle the things that begin with the q sound.

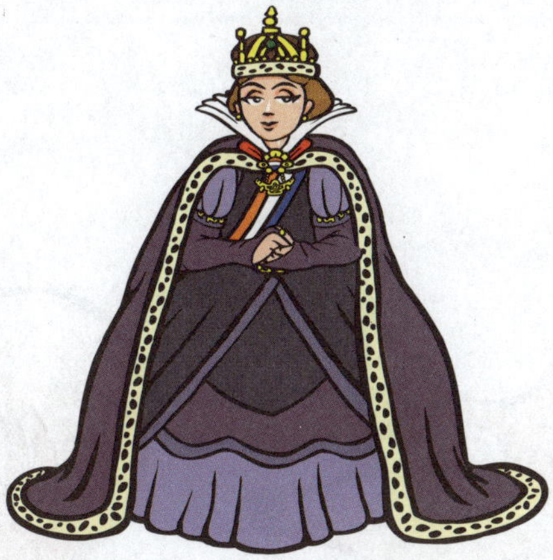

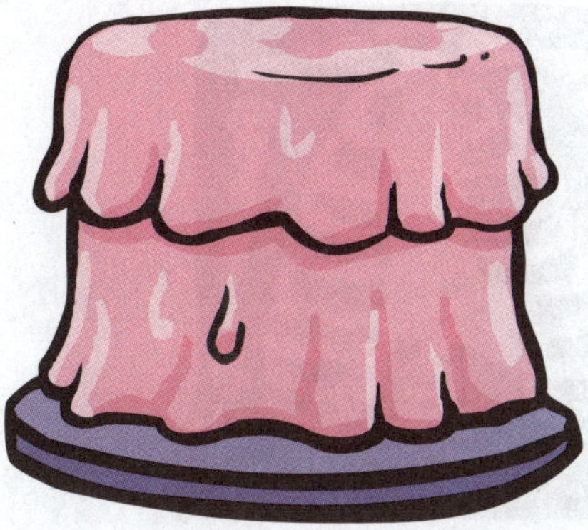

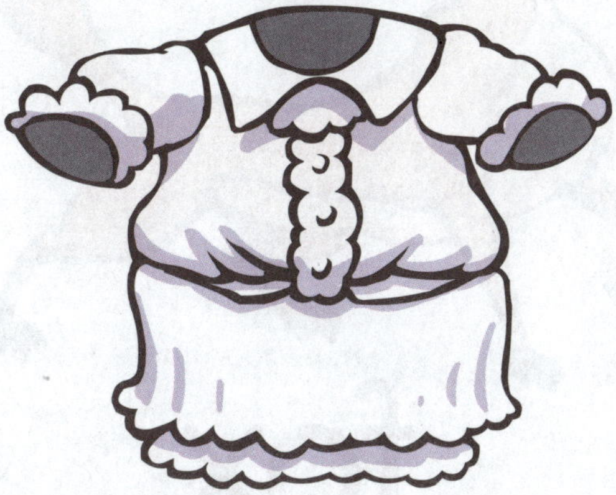

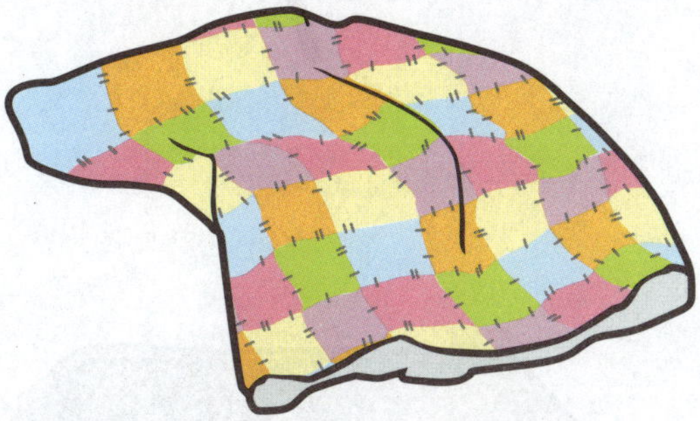

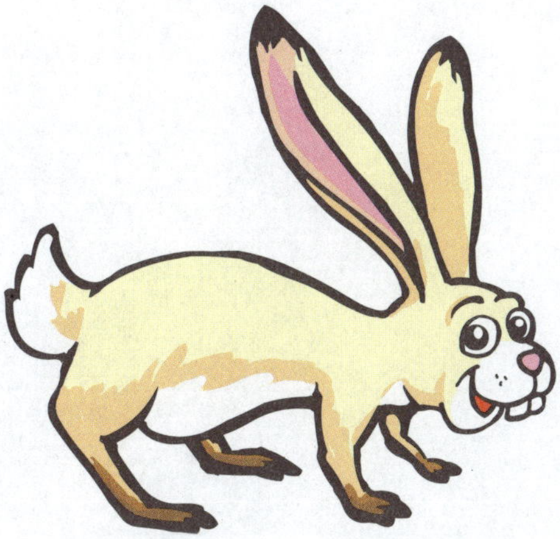

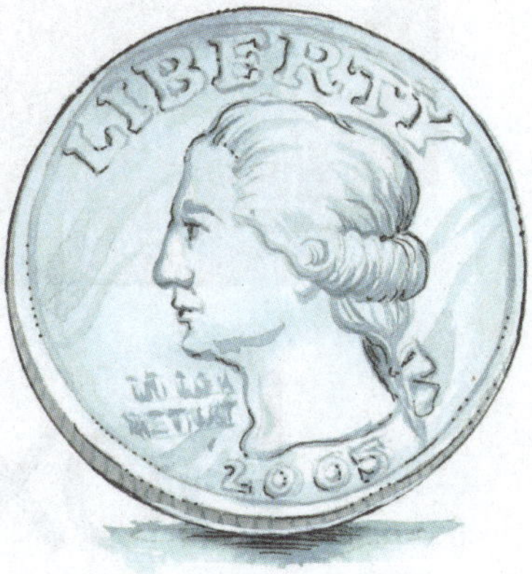

Look at the pictures. Point to the letter "x."
Listen for the x sound as you say each word out loud.

box

Exciting x

Say the name of each thing out loud.
Circle the things that end with an **x** sound.

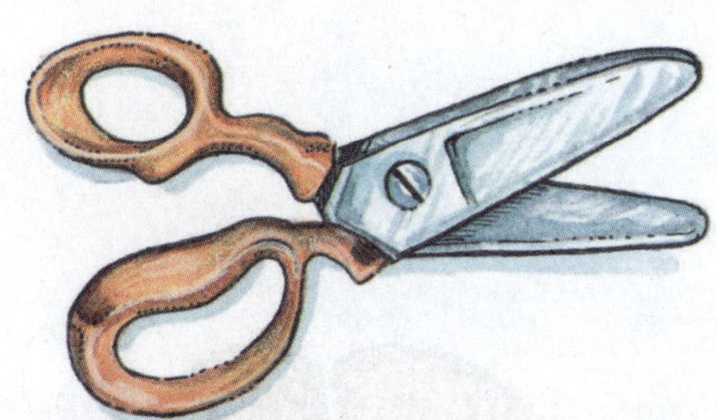

Look at the pictures. Point to the letter "y."
Listen for the y sound as you say each word out loud.

yo-yo

yawn

yarn

Yappy y

Say the name of the things in each row out loud.
Circle the thing that begins with the y sound.

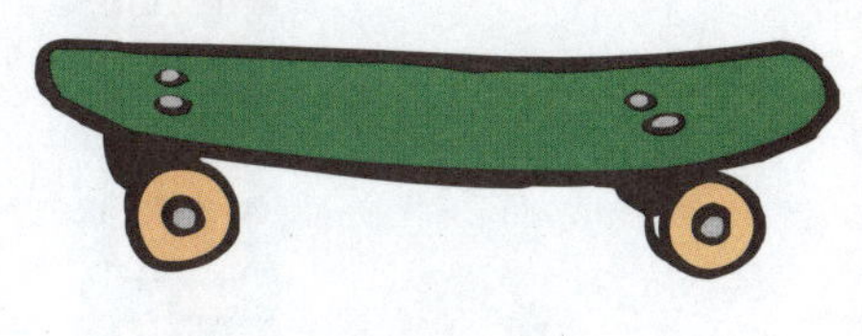

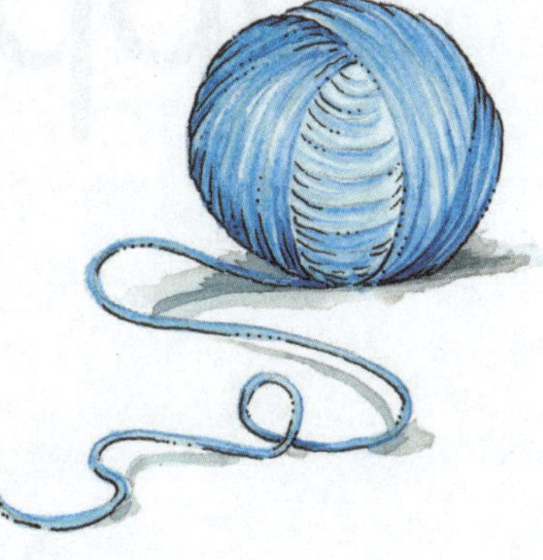

Look at the pictures. Point to the letter "z."
Listen for the z sound as you say each word out loud.

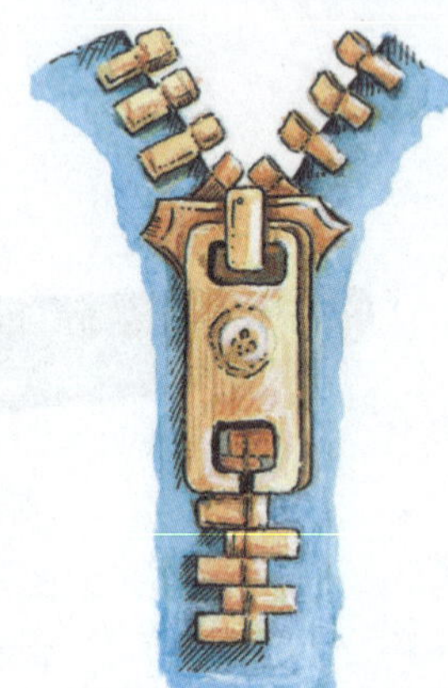

zipper

zebra

zoo

Zippy z

Say the name of each thing out loud.
Circle the things that begin with the z sound.

Sound Roundup

Circle the letter that matches the beginning sound of each thing.

r t v

r t v

r t v

r t v

What's That Sound?

Say the names of the things in each row out loud. Circle the thing that begins or ends with the letter sound.

q

x

y

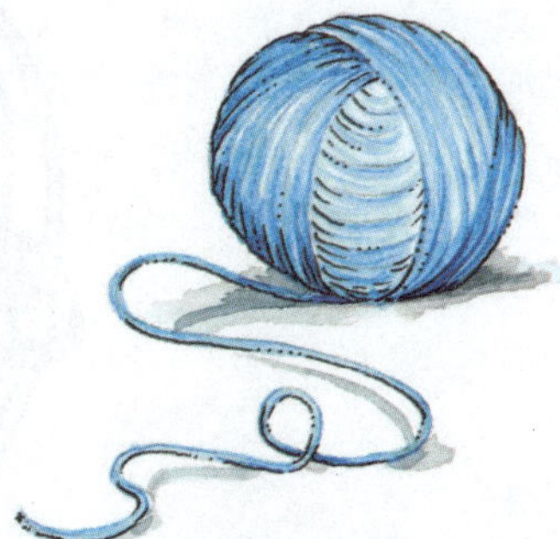

z

Look at the pictures.
Point to the letter "a" in their names.
Listen for the short a sound as you say each word out loud.

Always a

Color the things with the short a sound as in cat.

Look at the pictures.
Point to the letter "i" in their names.
Listen for the short **i** sound as you say each word out loud.

igloo

pig

fish

Interesting i

Help Hip-O get to the igloo.
Draw a path through the things with the short **i** sound as in **win**.

Look at the pictures.
Point to the letter "o" in their names.
Listen for the short o sound as you say each word out loud.

Only o

Say the name of each thing out loud.
Circle each thing that has the short o sound as in pot.

u

Look at the pictures.
Point to the letter "u" in their names.
Listen for the short **u** sound as you say each word out loud.

umbrella

sun

drum

Unusual u

Say the name of each picture out loud.
Color the things with the short **u** sound as in **sun**.

e

Look at the pictures.
Point to the letter "e" in their names.
Listen for the short e sound as you say each word out loud.

Excellent e

Say the name of each picture out loud.
Circle the things that have the short e sound as in pet.

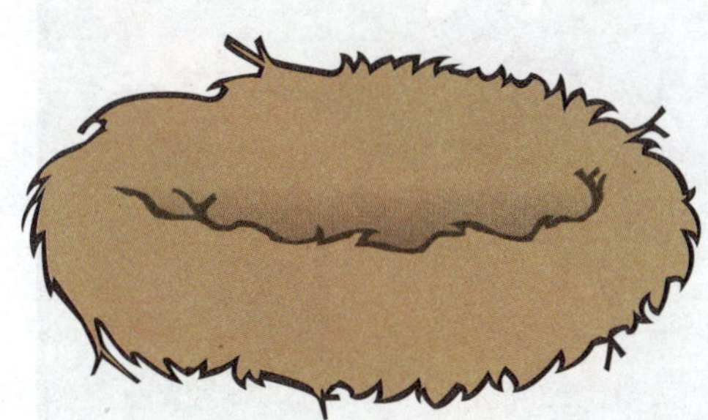

The Alphabet Party

Ant bit a carrot.

Dog and Elephant found a goat.

Horse invited a juggler.

Kangaroo and Lizard munched noodles.

Octopus paraded with the Queen Bee.

The rabbits sipped tea under the violets.

Whale and Fox played with yo-yos.

Zebra zoomed in!

I did it!

Congratulations!

has successfully completed this workbook.